MARiA OROSA

FREEDOM FiGHTER, SCiENTiST AND iNVENTOR
FROM THE PHiLiPPiNES

NORMA OLiZON-CHiKiAMCO

ILLUSTRATRATED BY

MARK SALVATUS

TUTTLE Publishing

Tokyo | Rutland, Vermont | Singapore

Published by Tuttle Publishing, an imprint of
Periplus Editions (HK) Ltd.

www.tuttlepublishing.com

Library of Congress Cataloging-in-
Publication Data is in process.

ISBN: 978-0-8048-5532-7

First edition
25 24 23 22   5 4 3 2 1

Printed in China   2211EP

Distributed by

**North America, Latin America
& Europe**
Tuttle Publishing
364 Innovation Drive
North Clarendon
VT 05759-9436, USA
Tel: 1 (802) 773 8930
Fax: 1 (802) 773 6993
info@tuttlepublishing.com
www.tuttlepublishing.com

Japan
Tuttle Publishing
Yaekari Building 3rd Floor
5-4-12 Osaki
Shinagawa-ku
Tokyo 141-0032
Tel: (81) 3 5437-0171
Fax: (81) 3 5437-0755
sales@tuttle.co.jp
www.tuttle.co.jp

Asia Pacific
Berkeley Books Pte. Ltd.
3 Kallang Sector #04-01
Singapore 349278
Tel: (65) 67412178
Fax: (65) 67412179
inquiries@periplus.com.sg
www.tuttlepublishing.com

"Books to Span the East and West"

Tuttle Publishing was founded in 1832 in the small New England town of Rutland,
Vermont [USA]. Our core values remain as strong today as they were then—to publish
best-in-class books which bring people together one page at a time. In 1948, we established a
publishing office in Japan—and Tuttle is now a leader in publishing English-language books
about the arts, languages and cultures of Asia. The world has become a much smaller place
today and Asia's economic and cultural influence has grown. Yet the need for meaningful
dialogue and information about this diverse region has never been greater. Over the past
seven decades, Tuttle has published thousands of books on subjects ranging from martial
arts and paper crafts to language learning and literature—and our talented authors,
illustrators, designers and photographers have won many prestigious awards. We welcome
you to explore the wealth of information available on Asia at **www.tuttlepublishing.com**.

CONTENTS

Born...Just Before a Revolution

Maria Ylagan Orosa was born on November 29, 1893 in Taal. She was the fourth of the eight children of Juliana Ylagan y de Castro and Simplicio Orosa y Agoncillo.

Simplicio was a sea captain. The family also owned a general store in the town of Bauan.

It was a time of great change in the Philippines. Spain's rule of the country was coming to an end. But the United States soon took control. The Filipinos resisted. They formed groups to fight the Americans. To help, Simplicio carried supplies and soldiers on his steamboat. But the Americans found out and arrested Simplicio.

While he was in jail, his son Sixto brought him meals. Years later, Maria would bravely feed prisoners too.

Simplicio passed away in 1910. Maria's mother was left to raise her children and to run the store.

Adventure on the High Seas

After high school, Maria pursued her love of science. She studied pharmacy at the University of the Philippines. But after a year, she set off on her next great adventure. Along with two friends, she sailed for the United States aboard a Japanese steamship.

After many weeks at sea, they arrived in Washington on August 18, 1916.

Living in the USA

Life for a foreign student in America was not easy. While studying at the University of Washington, Maria worked many different jobs. She picked fruit in orchards. She washed dishes in restaurants and cleaned houses. She even worked in a canning factory in Alaska.

To save money she wore hand-me-downs. Her winter coats were too big or too small. She would laugh about her clothes that didn't fit. But she never lost sight of her dreams.

While studying chemistry, Maria still helped with the family store back in the Philippines. Many of her letters home were about the orders from American department stores. They ordered baby bibs, straw bags, handkerchiefs and hats. Maria would send the money home to her mother.

A good student, Maria soon received an offer she couldn't refuse. The dean of the College of Pharmacy wanted her to work at his food laboratory. As the state's food inspector, he made her his assistant. She tested dairy products, sugar, vinegar and fruits.

Maria Earns Her Degrees

Maria was a born scientist. She was curious about the world around her. She asked questions. Then she set out to find the answers.

Maria had a great talent for chemistry. Given a scholarship by the Philippine government, she earned two degrees—in 1917 and 1918—in food science and pharmacy.

She was just getting started. Maria was soon named assistant state chemist. Then in 1921 she earned a master's degree in pharmacy. It was now official: Maria was a scientist!

Maria's Magical Inventions

It was time for Maria to head home. At first she worked at a university. She taught her students cooking and how to run a household. Then she worked as a chemist at the Bureau of Science. Traveling around the country, she and her team taught women about good nutrition.

Maria then returned to the United States to study canning and preserving food. Back in the Philippines she became head of the country's food preservation office.

The work Maria did was like magic! She gave new life to mangoes, pineapples and jackfruits. She canned and bottled them. She turned them into jams and jellies.

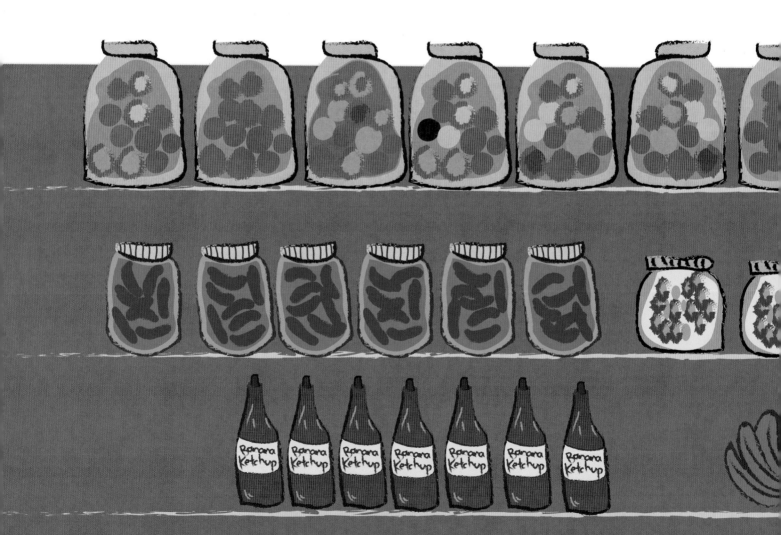

At the time, canned foods were mostly imported. They were pricey too. So Maria's fruits and vegetables became a hit.

She used local food in new ways. She turned cassava, a root vegetable, into flour. She made vinegar out of pineapples and ketchup out of bananas. Soon banana ketchup became used in nearly every Filipino home.

Maria's helpers were called Orosa's Girls. Together they came up with recipes for vegetables like *alugbati* and for wild shrubs and herbs such as *chaya* and *talinum*. They created over 300 recipes for coconuts alone.

They also found new uses for soybeans and rice bran. Known as *darak*, it was fed to pigs and horses. But Maria knew it was rich in vitamin B. So she turned it into cookies, cakes and muffins.

Maria also invented the *palayok* or clay oven, which offered women a healthy way to cook without electricity.

Saving Lives—with Cookies

In December 1941, the Japanese invaded the Philippines. Again the Filipinos fought back.

While still working as a scientist, Maria became an undercover agent! She passed along secret messages and gave money to groups fighting the Japanese. She became a captain in a group called Marking's Guerillas. The soybean powder she invented gave fuel to the fighters and fed the sick and hungry.

Maria also sneaked food into the camps where starving prisoners were being held. She even hid packets of food inside hollow bamboo tubes. The tubes were brought to the camps by men pretending to be construction workers. The food would then be handed out to the prisoners.

freedom

Sometimes Sixto Orosa brought food to the prisoners. *Calamansi* juice and *darak* cookies made by Maria gave them strength. These foods were rich in Vitamin C and other nutrients.

For a taste of Maria's *darak* cookies, see the recipe on page 32.

She Was All That....and More!

Maria's family knew her best. Her niece Rosalinda admired Maria's drive and hard work.

Another niece, Helen, would often visit Maria in her office. They fondly called her Tia (Aunt) Mary. One day, after greeting Maria, Helen started to cry. Maria told her to be hopeful as the end of the war seemed near.

"I feel privileged to have shared with her in whatever happiness—it must have been precious little!—she might have had during those ....days of ....fear, real risk and danger."

At work Maria was kind and generous. She would remember clerks and janitors on their birthdays and would take food and money to sick employees.

While Maria's brother Jose was studying in Seattle, he would always drop by her lab in time for lunch because she would always feed him.

Rosalinda L. Orosa

Jose's daughter Milette remembers her father's words: "She was generous not only to him but to all the Filipino students. She was the first to find out that working in the canning factories in Alaska paid well. Dad said she encouraged the Filipino students to work there, too, during summer. They would all go back to Seattle very happy with their wallets full."

Maria spent her life helping others. She often had little or no money. "What if you get ill?" her mother asked her. Maria answered, "I can always go to a public hospital."

Milette Orosa

Helen Orosa del Rosario

Alice Orosa Tigno

Jose Y. Orosa

Her niece Alice remembers that in the Orosa house, Maria planted *kamias* and *santol* trees. She preserved the fruit in glass jars.

Maria never looked for praise. "If you called her a heroine to her face, if she were alive today and you did that, she'd laugh at you," her friend Yay Panlilio wrote.

Maria Y. Orosa

Braving the Dangers

As the war drew on, Manila became more and more dangerous. Maria was warned to get out of the city. Her brother Sixto begged her to join his family in Batangas. There they would be safer.

But Maria refused to leave. She was "a soldier and soldiers do not abandon their post." "My place is here," she said. "I cannot abandon my work and my girls."

"I remember the last time I saw her," Rosalinda recalls. "We were leaving at dawn, and my aunt, so as not to miss seeing us off, had rushed down the stairs, forgetting to put on her lounging robe. There she stood in her pajamas, a sweet smile on her face, her chubby hand waving at us."

In the Line of Duty

Maria kept working despite the dangers. Japanese soldiers threatened her, but she carried on with her work.

When American forces arrived to fight the Japanese, they bombed Manila. On February 13, 1945, Maria's lab was struck. She was rushed to the hospital where she died.

Back at the Orosa house, news of Maria's death stunned her family. "Everyone was crying," Alice recalls.

Maria was buried in a mass grave along with other war victims. In 2020, a gravestone with her name on it was found in the yard of the Malate Catholic School. Along the bottom were the words "Died in line of duty."

MARIA Y. OROSA ST.

To
Maria Y. Orosa
For Service
the American
National
Red Cross

A Grateful Nation Honors Maria

To honor Maria, a street in Manila was named after her. She was also given a humanitarian award by the American Red Cross and a Presidential Medal of Merit by the Philippine government.

A monument in her hometown and a plaque at the Bureau of Plant Industry also pay tribute to this scientist who helped others.

In the Philippines and around the world, Maria's memory lives on, inspiring young scientists today. Smart and brave, she's remembered as the war hero, inventor and chemist who saved many lives and helped to feed a nation.

Maria's Freedom Cookies

These cookies saved many lives in the Philippines during World War II. As such they are almost sacred. They symbolize the struggle of the Filipinos for freedom, and the bravery of Maria Y. Orosa, who helped feed a starving nation during the war. Today we can call them the Orosa Freedom Cookies in honor of her courage and dedication.

½ cup (115 g) butter

⅓ cup (75 g) sugar

½ cup (70 g) rice bran or *tiki tiki* flour

½ cup (70 g) all-purpose flour

1 egg, well beaten

Grated rind from half a lime

Additional butter, for brushing

Preheat the oven to 350°F (180°C). In the bowl of an electric mixer, cream the butter until fluffy. Gradually add the sugar, rice bran, all-purpose flour, egg and grated rind.

Brush two cookie sheets with butter. Scoop the dough, about 1 teaspoon per cookie, placing it about 2 inches (10 cm) apart on a greased cookie sheet. Bake in the preheated oven for nine to ten minutes, or until the edges of the cookies start to brown.

Let the cookies rest about one to two minutes then transfer them to a cooling rack. Makes about 30 cookies. Store any leftovers in an airtight container.

Sources

Orosa.org: I Remember My Father, by Dr. Sixto Y.Orosa.

The Recipes of Maria Y. Orosa, with Essays on Her life and Work: Compiled and Edited by Helen L. Orosa del Rosario.

The Woman Who Was Maria Y. Orosa by Rosalinda L. Orosa.

The Science Educator: A Selfless Life: Maria Y. Orosa.

Maria Ylagan Orosa: Freedom Fighter and Food Chemist: Women's Journal, November 29, 1975.

Maria Y. Orosa by Yay Panlilio.

Arts and Mind: Maria Y. Orosa, War Heroine, Master of Culinary Arts by Leonor Orosa Goquingco, Manila Bulletin, December 11, 1998.

Official Gazette of the Republic of the Philippines, July 1949.

The Search for Maria Orosa and Other Victims of the 1945 Bombing of Remedios Hospital, Kristine Sabillo, ABS-CBN News.

Orosa.org. Reminiscences I: Growing up in the Philippines by Mario E. Orosa.

Maria Christina Diding Orosa (+).

Amazing Filipino Women Heroes, Philippine Veterans Affairs Office, Department of National Defense.

Lady Science: Maria Ylagan Orosa and the Chemistry of Resistance.

Acknowledgements

This book was made possible with the help and encouragement of several people, to whom I would like to express my profound gratitude.

For providing me with valuable sources of information as well as interesting details of Maria Y. Orosa's life, I am truly grateful to members of the distinguished Orosa clan, particularly:

Dr. Sixto Y. Orosa Sr. (+)
Helen L. Orosa del Rosario (+)
Jose Y. Orosa (+)
Maria Christina Orosa (+)
Rosalinda L. Orosa
Mario E. Orosa
Evelyn Orosa del Rosario Garcia
Chic Orosa del Rosario Francisco
Elaine Orosa del Rosario Lim
Milette Orosa
Alice Orosa Tigno
Melanie Naylor

A big thanks to my publishers Tuttle Publishing and Periplus, and their staff, for believing in this project, and for their patience in seeing this book to its finish:

Eric Oey
Doug Sanders
Anthoney Chua
Sheryll Tacuban Taghap
Anthony Tabilla
Ann Niklasson
Christopher Johns
Brandy LaMotte
C.J. Regala Casuga

And to Mark Salvatus, for his beautiful illustrations in this book.

I am also extremely grateful to my family Calixto, Pia and Clarissa, for their loving encouragement, and for being there for me, always.